Coastal Lowland
Wildflowers

J.E. (Ted) Underhill

hancock

house

ISBN 0-88839-973-1

Canadian Cataloging in Publication Data

Underhill, J.E., 1919—
Coastal lowland wildflowers

(Wildflower series)
Bibliography: p.
Includes Index.
ISBN 0-88839-973-1

1. Wild flowers — British Columbia —
Identification. 2. Wild flowers — Northwest, Pacific
— Identification. 3. Coastal flora — British
Columbia — Identification. 4. Coastal flora —
Northwest, Pacific — Identification.
I. Title. II. Series.
QK203.B7U54 1985   582.13'09711   C84-091579-9

Edited by Diana Ottosen
Typeset by Elizabeth Grant and Jaine Bruce
Layout/production by Dorothy Forbes

Front cover photos: Washington coast "beach log zone."
                                    Pacific Dogwood
Back cover photo: Viola orbiculata

Printed in Hong Kong

Published simultaneously in Canada and the United States by

HANCOCK HOUSE PUBLISHERS LTD.
19313 Zero Ave., Surrey, B.C. V3S 5J9
HANCOCK HOUSE PUBLISHERS INC.
1431 Harrison Avenue, Blaine, WA 98230

INTRODUCTION

Spring comes to the Pacific Northwest riding on the year's first warm, gentle winds that blow in off the Pacific in late February or early March.

All along the coast the wildflowers begin to stir, beginning their annual round of activity. Amongst the first to rouse, near my place, are the Yellow Arums in the boggy hollows, and Satin Flowers on the rock bluffs. By our back fence a shrub of Indian Plum hangs out its white blossoms. These first plants, whatever they may be, are a signal to us that the time is at hand to cast off the lethargy of winter, to don boots and jacket, and to get out and enjoy spring's flower show.

This is a book about the more conspicuous of the wildflowers that you are apt to find between the coast and the Cascades from about central Oregon north to the Skeena River in B.C. The book deals primarily with plants which grow along the coast and in the lowland valleys. Some of these, however, continue to grow up to quite high levels in the mountains. Such plants are marked as occurring in upland areas. There are other species, usually those of the coastal rock bluffs, which occur in the arid inland sagebrush country. These are marked as occurring in sagebrush areas. A few species also grow high on the mountains between timberline and peak. These plants are marked as occurring in alpine areas.

In a general sense this coastal strip is characterized by mild temperatures and abundant rainfall. Nurtured by these, the land has produced one of the most magnificent softwood forests in the world. We who live here are apt to forget this fact. It is hard to stand in Portland or Seattle or Vancouver, B.C. and comprehend that our great-great-grandfathers saw majestic forests where we see huge, sprawling cities.

But not all of the coastland has the same climate, nor has it all produced great forests. The most notable exception is a large area within the Puget Sound/Strait of Georgia basin. Air reaching this area from the Pacific must for the most part flow over the Olympics or the mountains of Vancouver Island. During this forced rise the air is cooled so that much of its moisture content falls on the western slopes and by the time it reaches Puget Sound and the Strait of Georgia the air is relatively dry. This drier area is what is aptly termed a "rain-shadow." Victoria, B.C., the northeastern part of the Olympic Peninsula, and most of the Gulf Islands are clearly in the rain-shadow, and around its edges there is a wide band which is affected to a lesser degree. To give you an idea of the significance of the rain-shadow, the annual rainfall at Hoh River in Washington and at many other places along the exposed coast is in excess of 140 inches (356 cm.), while the annual total at Victoria, B.C. is about 30 inches (76 cm.), and some places have less. This explains why some plants of the rain-shadow, such as *Sisyrinchium douglasii* and *Lithophragma parviflora*, also occur in the sagebrush country of the interior.

As you read the individual plant descriptions in this book, you will soon see that there are four principal habitat-types whose plants are listed here. They are (1) the driftwood zone at the tops of the beaches; (2) open, mossy rock outcrops; (3) open grassy meadows—which may be very small; and (4) coast forest—in a general sense. Each of these types of places has a unique set of growing conditions and is inhabited by plants which are adapted to those conditions. This can help you when you seek to identify a strange plant.

In this and other books in this series, the English names used are principally those chosen by Lewis J. Clark in his books. It must be realized that there are no English names for plants in the form of a standard international list. Some plants go by quite a few common names in the various parts of their range.

The word "herb" may puzzle some readers. Its meaning here is that listed in the *Concise Oxford Dictionary*: "a plant of which the stem is not woody or persistent, and which dies down to the ground after flowering."

This, of course, is not a book for the serious botanist, but one for the non-specialist who wants to be able to put a name to the more showy plants he or she spots along the way. For this reason, the plants are grouped by their flower color, then are further grouped to bring together the ones which look similar or which grow together in the same habitat. Some plants are variable in color, and these are normally placed in the color section which best represents them.

As you walk or drive near the coast in search of wildflowers, you will perhaps get the impression that they are far scarcer here than in, say, the alpine. I don't think this is really the case. In the short alpine summer everything must rush into bloom and seed within a few short weeks, and there is little time for the plants to produce a lot of green growth. Near the coast, on the other hand, where the growing season is longer, there is much more time. Plants can usually be blooming profusely by March, and they have reasonably good growing conditions for at least five months, so there's no need to hurry. The plants have ample time to produce the leafiness they need to survive if they live in the shade of big trees, and then flower and seed. You just do not see the vivid two-week show that you might above timberline. The exception, of course, is to be found on the mossy rock bluffs near the coast. Here the season is brief, for summer drought dries the thin soil and moss by about June. On certain bluffs therefore, you can find wonderful carpets of color for a brief time in spring.

Of all the wildflowers of the Pacific Northwest, those near the coast are probably suffering most from civilization. Our homes, roads and parking lots have already exterminated wildflowers over hundreds of square miles. People who pick them are exterminating even more, because many of the species are irreparably harmed by picking. And they are not suited to the soils or culture of the home garden. Learn to know and enjoy the wildflowers—but leave them for all to enjoy!

REDBERRY ELDER
Sambucus racemosa

- shrub, usually 6 to 9 feet (2 to 3 m.)
- roadsides and clearings in coastal valleys
- leaves compound, with lance-like, toothed leaflets

The racemes of tiny white flowers are followed by bunches of small scarlet berries. Birds relish them, but they taste foul to most people.

INDIAN PLUM (Osoberry)
Osmaronia cerasiformis

- shrub, usually 6 to 9 feet (2 to 3 m.)
- common in coastal thickets and ditch banks
- leaves notably bright green, wavy-edged

Indian plum is first of our native shrubs to blossom here in Victoria, B.C. The little purple "plums" seldom ripen, because the birds avidly consume them at an earlier stage.

OCEAN SPRAY
Holodiscus discolor

Also found in sagebrush areas

- shrub, usually 6 to 9 feet (2 to 3 m.)
- forest edge and open ground
- leaves thin, broadly lance-like, strongly veined, toothed

Big arching sprays of tiny creamy-white flowers often bloom en masse on these shrubs to make a showy display. Soon, however, Ocean Spray turns a dingy brown.

THIMBLEBERRY
Rubus parviflorus

Also found in upland areas

- shrub, usually 3 to 6 feet (1 to 2 m.)
- widespread on roadsides and forest edge
- leaves large, soft, deeply-veined, lobed, toothed

This relative of Wild Raspberry bears a red fruit that is sweet but insipid. However, it is pleasant-tasting mixed with other berries. The canes lack prickles, and often have galls caused by small insects.

STINK CURRANT
Ribes bracteosum

- shrub, usually 6 to 9 feet (2 to 3 m.)
- streambanks and moist forest glades
- leaves maple-like, lobed, toothed, prominently veined

As the name suggests, the plant has a rank and obnoxious smell. The fruit, too, is unpleasant and makes some people ill.

W. MERILEES

GOATSBEARD

Aruncus sylvester

Also found in upland areas

- herb, usually 3 to 6 feet (1 to 2 m.)
- moist forest edge, coast to mid elevations
- leaves compound, leaflets lance-like with teeth on teeth

Observe this plant closely and you'll note that there are separate male and female plants, and that their flowers differ.

VANILLA LEAF
Achlys triphylla

- herb, usually about 12 inches (30 cm.)
- moist forests west of the Cascades
- one big leaf divided into 3 wavy-edged leaflets

Achlys leaves have a strong vanilla odor that is reputed to drive off flies. Notice that the tiny flowers consist primarily of tufts of white stamens.

FALSE BUGBANE
Trautvettaria caroliniensis

- herb, from 2 to 4½ feet (70 to 150 cm.)
- moist forest edge and glades
- leaves large, deeply-lobed, and toothed

Look closely; there are no petals, and the flower is made showy only by its mass of white stamens as is *Achlys*, which likely grows nearby.

W. MERILEES

FALSE SOLOMON SEAL
Smilacina racemosa

Also found in upland areas

- herb, usually 2 to 3 feet (60 to 90 cm.)
- moist forest edge and glades
- leaves large, parallel-veined

Older plants are quite spectacular with a cluster of several to many leafy stems, each holding aloft its big white panicle of flowers.

HIMALAYA BERRY
Rubus procerus

- vigorous sprawling perennial to 9 feet (3 m.)
- wasteland in coastal lowlands and valleys
- leaves compound, leaves and stems armed

Luther Burbank developed this plant for horticultural use. It quickly jumped the fences to become a weed, and was replaced by the Loganberry and Merionberry which were superior commercially.

WHITE MORNING GLORY
Convolvulus sepium

- vigorous sprawling vine
- wasteland and gardens, wide-spread
- leaf shape variable, often halberd-shaped

If our gardens can receive a curse, it is surely this plant from Eurasia. It spreads efficiently by deep rhizomes and by ample seed. The smaller *C. arvensis* is a lesser pest.

BIGROOT (Manroot)
Marah oreganus

- vigorous trailing vine
- sporadic on dry, open coastal slopes
- leaves large, shallowly lobed, with pointed teeth

As with other kinds of melons, there are separate and different male and female flowers. The fruit in this species is almost smooth. Further south are several spiny-fruited kinds.

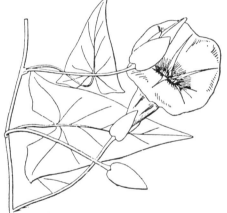

LARGE WHITE TRILLIUM
Trillium ovatum

- herb, usually 8 to 12 inches (20 to 30 cm.)
- moist coastal woodlands to the Cascades
- usually 3 leaves, very broad and pointed

Trillium's flowers are usually white, aging to pink or wine-red. Picking usually kills the plant, and it is thus protected by law in British Columbia.

WHITE FAWN LILY (Easter lily, Curly lily, Trout lily)

Erythronium oregonum

- herb, usually 6 to 12 inches (15 to 30 cm.)
- woodlands and meadows, especially in the "rain-shadow"
- leaves long, smooth, mottled dark brown

Here, surely, is an example of a plant with a confusing array of common names! *Erythroniums* occur in some variety from British Columbia to California. Some kinds often occur in spectacular masses. Shown below is a portion of the churchyard of St. Mary the Virgin at Metchosin, B.C. Many people come here in early April to admire the white fawn lilies.

LARGE-LEAVED SANDWORT
Arenaria macrophylla

- herb, usually about 2 to 3 inches (5 to 8 cm.)
- dryish, open forest—both sides of the Cascades
- leaves lance-like, opposite, thin

This is quite unlike most of our *Arenarias* which tend to be low, tufted plants with very narrow, linear leaves, found in open places.

LYALL'S ANEMONE
Anemone lyallii

- herb, usually 4 to 8 inches (10 to 20 cm.)
- open forest, coast to the Cascades
- 3 leaves, each with 3 toothed leaflets

Many people miss this fragile woodlander because it's small and its color is gentle. You must stop and look closely to fully appreciate its beauty.

FALSE LILY-OF-THE-VALLEY

Maianthemum dilatatum

- herb, usually about 8 inches (20 cm.)
- moist open forest, west of the Cascades
- usually 2 leaves, heart-shaped, parallel-veined

This does considerably resemble true Lily-Of-The-Valley *Convallaria majalis,* but has less scent, and bears its few blossoms and berries right around its stalk. *Convallaria* is distinctly one-sided.

WESTERN SPRING BEAUTY
Montia sibirica

- herb, usually 3 to 5 inches (5 to 12 cm.)
- moist woodlands, widespread
- leaves usually lance-like, fleshy and smooth, but variable

The flowers are usually white, sometimes pale pink, and often marked with red stripes. The tips of the petals are notched.

MINERS' LETTUCE
Montia perfoliata

- herb, extremely variable, to about 12 inches (30 cm.)
- well-drained, seasonally moist, open places
- lower leaves lance-like, smooth

This species is distinguished by its upper leaves which are usually joined to form a disc above which the small flowers are borne.

EARLY SAXIFRAGE
Saxifraga integrifolia

Also found in upland and sagebrush areas

- herb, variable, to about 16 inches (40 cm.) at maturity
- mossy rock bluffs and short-grass slopes
- leaves basal, broad, blunt, often rusty-haired beneath

The photo shows a typical coastal form at the bud stage. Notice the red hairiness on the stem.

YELLOW-LEAVED IRIS
Iris chrysophylla

- herb, usually about 6 inches (15 cm.)
- sandy woodland edge near the coast
- leaves linear, parallel-veined

This is but one of a variety of small *Iris* species that may be found along the coast from central Oregon southwards in late spring. See also *I. douglasiana* on p. 57.

WILD STRAWBERRY
Fragaria vesca

- herb, to about 6 inches (15 cm.)
- dry, open ground, coast to east of the Cascades
- leaves compound, with 3 toothed leaflets

We have three Wild Strawberry species native to our area. The commonest coastal species, *F. chiloensis,* has rather thicker leaves and more rounded leaflets.

DEATH CAMAS
Zigadenus venenosus

Also found in sagebrush areas

- herb, usually 8 to 20 inches (20 to 50 cm.)
- coastal rock bluffs and grassy slopes
- leaves strap-like, long, yellow-green

Deadly poison bulbs of this species often grow with edible bulbs of true Camas (p. 58). Indians, for whom Camas was an important food, sometimes ate Death Camas with dire results.

MOUSE-EAR CHICKWEED
Cerastium arvense

Also found in sagebrush and alpine areas

- herb, mat-forming, to about 8 inches (20 cm.)
- rock bluffs and grassy meadows
- leaves gray-haired, narrow, usually lance-like

Deeply cleft petals and silvery foliage help to identify this handsome Chickweed. Away from the coast it can have a rather different appearance.

WILD CARROT
(Queen Anne's Lace)
Daucus carota

Also found in upland areas

- herb, usually 16 to 20 inches (40 to 50 cm.)
- widespread along roadsides and waste ground
- leaves finely divided

The cultivated Carrot of our vegetable gardens is said to have been developed from this species in the sixteenth century. Before that the small wild roots were used as medicine.

TALL FRINGE-CUP
Tellima grandiflora

- herb, to about 30 inches (80 cm.)
- moist open places on rich forest soils
- leaves mainly basal, maple-like, longstalked

You must look closely to enjoy the intricate design of the divided petals. The color is usually as shown, but tends to flush pink or reddish with age.

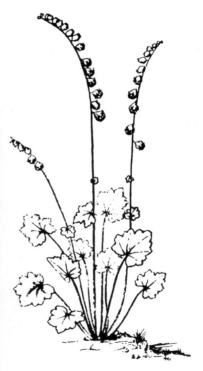

BROOM (Scotch Broom)
Cytisus scoparius

- shrub, to about 9 feet (3 m.)
- introduced and now common west of the Cascades
- leaves below with three leaflets

Broom arrived with settlers in the mid-1800's. Since then it has rapidly colonized open land, sometimes crowding out native species.

GORSE
Ulex europaeus

- shrub, usually 3 to 6 feet (1 to 2 m.)
- introduced and locally common west of the Cascades
- most of the leaves are modified as spines

Gorse, like Broom, is a member of the Pea family. The fragrant flowers of Gorse can usually be seen during much of the year.

TALL OREGON GRAPE
Berberis aquifolium

Also found in sagebrush areas

- shrub, usually 1½ to 4½ feet (45 to 150 cm.)
- common near the coast
- leaves "holly-like," mildly prickly

Note that the individual flower resembles in miniature that of a Daffodil. The berries make a good tart jelly for use with meats.

LARGE-LEAVED AVENS
Geum macrophyllum

- herb, usually 16 to 28 inches (40 to 70 cm.)
- forest edge and moist open ground
- basal leaves compound, with a large terminal leaflet

That unique basal leaf makes this *Geum* easy to identify. Otherwise it might easily be mistaken for a *Potentilla.*

WESTERN BUTTERCUP
Ranunculus occidentalis

- herb, usually about 1 foot (30 cm.)
- moist meadows near the coast
- lower leaves long-stalked, 3-lobed, toothed, hairy

A common and striking sight is a patch of this Buttercup highlighted with blue Camas. We have many Buttercup species.

W. MERILEES

TREE LUPINE
Lupinus arboreus

- shrub, from 3 to 6 feet (1 to 2 m.)
- sporadic near the coast
- leaves compound, somewhat hairy

Flower color of this species varies to white or bluish. We also have a variety of smaller Lupines. *L. bicolor,* a little blue and white type that grows above the beaches is specially attractive.

SPRING GOLD
Lomatium utriculatum

- herb, usually 8 to 16 inches (20 to 40 cm.) at maturity
- coastal rock bluffs and dry meadows
- leaves "carrot-like," much divided

Spring Gold opens its flowers in early stages of its growth while still close to the ground, but grows taller as the seed is matured. Yes, it is related to Carrot and Parsley.

YELLOW-EYED GRASS
Sisyrinchium californicum .

- herb, usually 6 to 12 inches (15 to 30 cm.)
- lakeshores and bogs near the coast
- leaves narrow

This is not a grass, despite the name, but a member of the Iris Family. Most of our *Sisyrinchiums* are in the purple to pink range. See page 30.

W. MERILEES

HAIRY CINQUEFOIL
Potentilla villosa

Also found in alpine areas

- herb, about 2 to 4 inches (5 to 10 cm.)
- crevices in coastal rock bluffs
- leaves with 3 leaflets, toothed, with hairy white edges

This beautiful little plant has adapted for life in a harsh environment. The hairiness on the leaves helps prevent water loss in hot sun, and probably also protects against salt spray.

LITTLE MONKEY FLOWER
Mimulus alsinoides

- herb, usually 2 to 6 inches (5 to 15 cm.)
- moist crevices and ledges on rock
- leaves small, broadly lance-like, and toothed

Large mats of this tiny annual often crowd the damp mossy seeps on coastal rock bluffs and make a brave show.

BROAD-LEAVED STONECROP
Sedum spathulifolium

- herb, to about 6 inches (15 cm.)
- common on rock bluffs near the coast
- leaves very fleshy, flattish and broad, in rosettes

Leaf color is extremely variable — from a glacial ice green to strong tints of red or purple. The plant's location has much to do with leaf color.

GUMWEED

Grindelia integrifolia

- herb, usually 12 to 24 inches (30 to 60 cm.)
- coastal beaches and lowland valleys
- basal leaves stalked, stem leaves often clasping

Gumweed is probably the most conspicuous plant of the beaches and salt marshes. Its name derives from the stickiness of the bracts beneath the flowers.

SILVER-WEED
Potentilla pacifica

- herb, usually 10 to 16 inches (25 to 40 cm.)
- beaches, marshes and streambanks
- leaves divided along a central rib, leaflets toothed

Silver-weed gets its name from the silver hairiness of the undersides of the leaves. This is even more apparent in *P. anserina* of the interior.

YELLOW SAND VERBENA
Abronia latifolia

- sprawling herb, stems to about 3 feet (90 cm.)
- driftwood zone of coastal beaches

Other than this yellow-flowered species, we have *A. umbellata* which has pink flowers and is another beach plant.

YELLOW ARUM
(Skunk cabbage)
Lysichitum americanum

- herb, leaves to 40 inches (100 cm.) or more
- swamps and streambanks
- leaves very large, broadly lance-like, soft

For many people this may be the first flower of spring as it blooms in February or March. Numerous tiny flowers are crowded on the central spadix.

WALL LETTUCE
Lactuca muralis

- herb, usually 1½ to 3 feet (45 to 90 cm.)
- moist coastal forests
- leaves large at the base, deeply lobed along midrib

Coastal lowlands have several kinds of *Lactuca*. This species is identified by its having so few (5) flowers in each little daisy head.

W. MERILEES

WOOD SORREL
Oxalis stricta

- herb, usually 12 to 16 inches (30 to 40 cm.)
- moist ground, especially western Washington
- leaves compound, "clover-like", with 3 leaflets

We have several yellow-flowered *Oxalis* species in the Pacific Northwest, some being serious weeds. There are also pink and white kinds.

CALIFORNIA POPPY
Eschscholtzia californica

- herb, usually about 12 to 16 inches (30 to 40 cm.)
- dry, sunny slopes
- leaves blue-green, much divided, succulent and fragile

California Poppy is sporadic along the coast in dry sites. Surely its most spectacular occurrence is the slope shown, on the west side of San Juan Island. When it is in bloom this patch is visible from Vancouver Island, about 8 miles away. Up close, the flowers are seen to occur in a variety of color forms other than the dominant orange. San Juan Island is overrun with rabbits, and they crop most succulent growth in open places. Apparently, however, California Poppy is not to their taste, so it thrives and the rabbits keep it free of competition.

Since the above was written, San Juan Island's rabbit population has crashed. Today the poppies are far fewer.

ORANGE HONEYSUCKLE
Lonicera ciliosa

- vine, sometimes climbing to 18 feet (6 m.)
- forests and thickets, widespread
- leaves blue-green, elliptic, soft

The uppermost leaf pairs are joined to form a disc or cup above which the flowers and the red berries are borne.

PINK RHODODENDRON
Rhododendron macrophyllum

Also found in upland areas

- shrub, usually 3 to 12 feet (1 to 4 m.)
- light forest, coast to Cascades
- leaves leathery, long, elliptic, smooth

This, the state flower of Washington, is certainly amongst the finest shrubs of the Pacific Northwest. It is scarce and slow-growing, and it should not be picked.

FLOWERING RED CURRANT
Ribes sanguineum

- shrub, from 3 to 9 feet (1 to 3 m.)
- forest edge and meadows
- leaves 3-lobed, toothed, heavily veined

Flower color varies from white to deep red, but the common form is rich pink. Selected forms are available at nurseries, and make good garden shrubs.

WILD ROSE

Rosa spp.

- shrubs, usually 3 to 6 feet (1 to 2 m.)
- ditch banks, forest edge, and clearings
- leaves compound, usually with 5 toothed, oval leaflets

We have several fairly similar species that make thickets by roadsides and behind beaches. In the forests is the smaller and fine-prickled *R. gymnocarpa.*

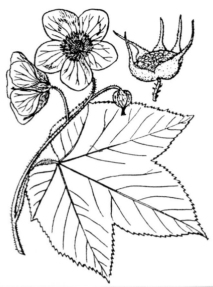

SALMON BERRY
Rubus spectabilis

- shrub, usually 6 to 9 feet (2 to 3 m.)
- streambanks, other moist places
- leaves compound, with 3 to 5 toothed leaflets

Fruit may be yellow, orange or dark red, and it is rather bland to the taste. Very rarely one may find a plant with fully double flowers.

HARDHACK
Spiraea douglasii

Also found in upland areas

- shrub, to about 6 feet (2 m.)
- marshes, streambanks, and pond edges
- leaves long-oval, with teeth on outer half

David Douglas, the Scottish botanist who explored much of the Pacific Northwest in the early 1800's, is honored in the name of this handsome shrub.

W. MERILEES

SALAL
Gaultheria shallon

Also found in upland areas

- shrub, usually 2 to 4 feet (60 to 120 cm.)
- moist forests, coast and mountain slopes
- leaves leathery, oval, pointed and finely toothed

David Douglas was excited to find this plant in 1825 and it was soon introduced to the gardens of England and Europe. The dark berries were a staple in the diet of some coastal Indians.

43

WESTERN BLEEDING HEART
Dicentra formosa

- herb, about 10 to 16 inches (25 to 40 cm.)
- moist forests, coast to the Cascades
- leaves blue-green, attractively divided, fragile

Look closely to appreciate the attractive and curiously shaped flowers, and their unusual smoky-rose color.

HEDGE NETTLE
Stachys cooleyae

- herb, usually 30 to 60 inches (75 to 150 cm.)
- moist thickets and woodland edge
- leaves lance-like, hairy, toothed and thin

The square stem and the flower shape help to place this as a member of the Mint Family. Despite its name, it is not related to the Stinging Nettle.

BEARBERRY (Kinnikinnik)
Arctostaphylos uva-ursi

Also found in upland and alpine areas

- trailing small shrub, making flat mats of growth
- rock bluffs and dry gravel, sun or semi-shade
- leaves evergreen, small, leathery, spoon-shaped

Bearberry colonies often form extensive mats of growth. In autumn these bear edible red berries. The species hybridizes freely with other *Arctostaphylos* species in our area.

PINK FAWN LILY
Erythronium revolutum

- herb, usually 6 to 10 inches (15 to 25 cm.)
- moist woodlands on alluvial soils
- leaves mottled with pallid lines, smooth

This species appears to be specially adapted to living in the silty soils of floodplains of some coastal streams and rivers.

FAIRY SLIPPER (Calypso)
Calypso bulbosa

- herb, usually 3 to 6 inches (8 to 15 cm.)
- rich, organic forest floor
- single leaf, oval, with prominent parallel veins

Calypso requires the special conditions of the forest to survive, perhaps depending upon a partnership with particular forest fungi. Picking or moving *Calypso* almost surely dooms the plant. Leave it for all to enjoy.

STARFLOWER
Trientalis latifolia

- herb, usually 4 to 8 inches (10 to 20 cm.)
- open moist woodlands
- leaves in a whorl, lance-like, not toothed

One to several flowers rise on short stalks above the leaf whorl. Color varies to deep pink or mauve. Starflower is related to *Primulas* of our gardens.

SEA BLUSH
Plectritis congesta

- herb, variably 2 to 16 inches (5 to 40 cm.)
- coastal rock bluffs, grassy places to the Cascades
- leaves opposite, held erect, blunt, not toothed

Like a number of other rock bluff species, this is an annual. It thus rests through the long summer droughts as seeds that do not require water.

BROAD-LEAVED SHOOTING STAR

Dodecatheon hendersonii

- herb, usually 4 to 12 inches (10 to 30 cm.)
- rock bluffs, short-grass meadows
- leaves broadly oval, smooth, held close to ground

The color is a bit variable, but the broad, flat leaves and the dark purple "snout" distinguish this from *D. pauciflorum* which has a yellowish snout and narrow, erect leaves.

NODDING ONION
Allium cernuum

Also found in upland and sagebrush areas

- **herb, usually 8 to 16 inches (20 to 40 cm.)**
- **widespread in dry sites**
- **several leaves, often forming clumps**

Nodding onion bulbs usually occur in a cluster at the soil surface. At the coast we also have *A. acuminatum* **with pink flowers held upright and sharp-tipped "petals."**

Allium acuminatum

BEACH PEA
Lathyrus japonicus

- clambering herb, usually 1 to 2 feet (30 to 60 cm.)
- above the logs on the shoreline
- leaves compound, with about 5 pairs of oval leaflets

Beach Pea is one of a group of plants specially suited to life on the beach. Near it watch for Gumweed (p. 33), Silver-weed (p. 34) and Yellow Sand Verbena (p. 34).

PERENNIAL PEA
Lathyrus latifolius

- climbing herb, often to 9 feet (3 m.)
- roadsides and waste ground near the coast
- leaves with 2 large leaflets and multiple tendrils

This pea, originally from Europe, escaped from garden confines long ago, and is well established as a wild plant. The heavily-winged stem is distinctive. Color varies to white.

PURPLE LOOSESTRIFE
Lythrum salicaria

- herb, usually 3 to 4½ feet (1 to 1.5 m.)
- marshes and damp, open places
- leaves usually opposite, lance-like, not toothed

Puget Sound area and southern Vancouver Island have large colonies of this plant introduced from Europe. There is a paler species, *L. hyssopifolia,* established further south.

ASTER
Aster hesperius

- herb, usually 20 to 36 inches (50 to 90 cm.)
- ditchbanks and waste ground
- leaves narrowly lance-like, of mixed sizes

Perhaps half a dozen *Aster* species grow near the coast. Flower color is usually in the mauve or mauve-pink range, and flowers bloom in late summer.

OYSTER PLANT (Salsify)
Tragopogon porrifolius

- herb, usually 2 to 3 feet (60 to 90 cm.)
- roadsides and waste ground
- leaves blue-green, narrow, stiff

In similar habitat you will also find the Yellow Oyster Plant, *T. dubius*. In both species the flowers are followed by big dandelion-like seed heads.

BITTER-SWEET
Solanum dulcamara

- clambering vine, to about 9 feet (3 m.)
- pond margins, other damp ground
- leaves extremely variable, often with 2 large basal lobes

The flowers are followed by berries that mature to a bright red and look like miniature Tomatoes—to which they are related. They are mildly poisonous and should not be eaten.

SATIN FLOWER
Sisyrinchium douglasii

Also found in sagebrush areas

- herb, usually 6 to 12 inches (15 to 30 cm.)
- rock bluffs and grassy knolls in the rain-shadow
- leaves many, narrow, sheathing the stem

On parts of the coast this is spring's first flower. It is rich purple on Vancouver Island, becoming redder to the south, and clear pink in sagebrush country.

DOUGLAS'S IRIS

Iris douglasiana

- herb, usually 1 to 2 feet (30 to 60 cm.)
- open, grassy coastal slopes
- leaves folded, narrow

Along the coast from Washington southwards the traveler may encounter several *Iris* species in a variety of combinations of white, yellow and mauve.

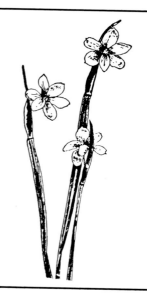

BLUE-EYED GRASS

Sisyrinchium angustifolium

Also found in upland and sagebrush areas

- herb, usually 6 to 12 inches (15 to 30 cm.)
- grassy meadows
- leaves narrow, flattened, sheathing the stem

This is an extremely variable and widespread plant species. It turns up in a variety of forms in the upland meadows and in sagebrush country.

CAMAS
Camassia quamash

- herb, usually 1 to 2 feet (30 to 60 cm.)
- grassy meadows, widespread
- leaves narrow, long, strap-like

We have two rather similar species: this, and C. *leichtlinii* which is taller and has other slight differences. Edible Camas bulbs were an important staple in the diet of some Indian groups.

Camassia leichtlinii

Camassia quamash and Valerianella congesta

MENZIES' LARKSPUR
Delphinium menziesii

- herb, usually 6 to 16 inches (15 to 40 cm.)
- coastal rock bluffs and grassy meadows
- leaves rounded in outline, but deeply lobed and dissected

The electric blue of *Wild Delphinium* sets it apart from our other native plants. We have a number of *Delphinium* species. Coastal forms usually have more leaf segments than shown here.

BLUE-EYED MARY
Collinsia grandiflora

Also found in upland areas

- herb, usually about 4 inches (10 cm.)
- coastal rock bluffs
- basal leaves rounded and toothed, stem leaves narrow

Collinsia is common on coastal rock bluffs, often growing with Sea Blush (p. 49). Look closely, and you can see that it is related to the Snapdragon of gardens.

SELF HEAL
Prunella vulgaris

- herb, usually 6 to 10 inches (15 to 25 cm.)
- forest edge and grassy meadows
- leaves lance-like, scarcely toothed

The crowded spike of small, hooded flowers is quite distinctive, although the flower color does vary to pink or white. The species is widespread.

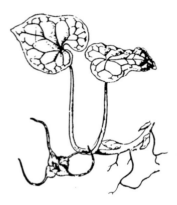

WILD GINGER
Asarum caudatum

Also found in upland areas

- herb, usually about 3 inches (8 cm.)
- moist forest floor, coast to mid-elevations
- leaves kidney-shaped and deeply veined

The beautiful and strange flowers, although quite large, are often hidden by the leaves and so go unnoticed by most people. A faint ginger smell provides the name.

CALIFORNIA PITCHER PLANT (Cobra Plant)
Darlingtonia californica

- herb, usually about 12 inches (30 cm.)
- swamps near central Oregon coast and southwards
- leaves hooded and mottled, "cobra-like"

The leaves are traps, baited within with a liquid which attracts insects, then digests their bodies. The actual flowers, not shown here, are reddish.

Fritillaria camschatcensis

CHOCOLATE LILY
Fritillaria lanceolata

Also found in upland areas

- herb, usually about 12 inches (30 cm.)
- grassy meadows, coast to mid-elevations
- leaves few, narrow, with a bluish cast

We have two species at the coast. *F. camschatcensis* is taller, leafier, and has flowers of a bell-like recurved shape in a darker, more solid color.

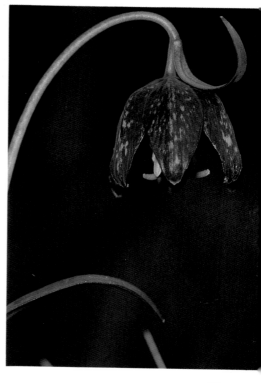

YOUTH-ON-AGE
Tolmiea menziesii

- herb, usually to about 24 inches (60 cm.)
- moist coastal forests
- leaves shallowly-lobed and unevenly toothed, hairy

The many people who buy this herb as a house plant seldom realize that it is common in the moist forests of the coastal valleys.

TWAYBLADE
Listera spp.

Also found in upland areas

- herbs, usually 3 to 8 inches (8 to 20 cm.)
- moist, mossy forest floor
- a single pair of opposite, oval leaves

These fragile little forest orchids are often come upon, but not as often noticed. We have several species, probably best distinguished by differences in the large "lip" petal.

INDEX

BIBLIOGRAPHY

BIANCHINI, F. and CORBETTA, F. Complete Book of Fruits and Vegetables, (New York: Crown Publishers, 1976).

CLARK, Lewis J. Wild Flowers of British Columbia, (Sidney, B.C.:Gray's Publishing, 1973).

HITCHCOCK, CRONQUIST, OWNBEY & THOMPSON Vascular Plants of the Pacific Northwest, (University of Washington Press, 1964).

LARRISON, PATRICK, BAKER & YAICH Washington Wildflowers, (Seattle Audubon Society, 1974).

NIEHAUS, T.F., and RIPPER, C.L. A Field Guide to Pacific States Wildflowers, (Boston: Houghton Mifflin Co., 1973).